EPHESIANS
Living Toward Eternity

Patricia H. Picardi

ChariotVICTOR
PUBLISHING
A DIVISION OF COOK COMMUNICATIONS

Victor Books is an imprint of ChariotVictor Publishing,
a division of Cook Communications, Colorado Springs, Colorado 80918
Cook Communications, Paris, Ontario
Kingsway Communications, Eastbourne, England

Editor: Carolyn Nystrom
Cover Design: Scott Rattray
Cover Photo: Derek Trask

Recommended Dewey Decimal Classification: 227.5
Suggested Subject Headings: BIBLE, N.T., EPHESIANS
ISBN: 1-56476-327-7

2 3 4 5 6 7 8 9 10 Printing/Year 99 98 97

Contents

Welcome to TruthSeed

I am a planter. Each spring finds me stooped in my garden, loose dirt churned soft by winter storms oozing into my worn sneakers, the smell of compost twitching my nose, warm sun thawing the muscles of my back, and precious seed — radish, carrots, lettuce, peas, beans, corn, beets, watermelon, cantaloupe, squash, cosmos, marigold, zinnia — trickling through my fingers. It's my favorite phase of gardening, one I try to remember as I tug at thick weeds in late June's humidity, swat mosquitoes in sweltering July twilight, and heft baskets of produce into my August-cluttered kitchen. I cut, peel, blanch, can, freeze, and (in recent years) mostly give away — with neighbors and coworkers cashing in on my penchant for planting. It's hard to believe that seeds barely filling a lunch bag spend a few weeks blending God's creative magic of sun, soil, and water into a winter's worth of food for a family. But that's what seed is all about. Abundant life encased in a tiny, hard shell.

No mere book can deliver full-grown, harvested produce — though some come close. Like seeds, books contain a grain of truth encased in the crusty shell of words. But plant that seed in the right season in a mind ready to learn, tug out the weeds of distraction that disrupt study, water it with a sweated-out attempt to put its truths into practice, invite with prayer the sunshine of God's grace, and expect a crop — enough to nurture personal growth, enough to give away.

What harvest can we expect from TruthSeed?

We can expect to know Scripture. Each book in this series invites us to explore either a topic addressed in several biblical passages or to study an entire book of the Bible. These are inductive studies. Each session leads us to explore a single passage on three levels: details of information presented in the text, accurate interpretation of that information, and personal response.

We can expect to experience God's presence. Scripture points us to God, its author and its object. It is His letter to us about Him-

4

self. As we read, study, and meditate on Scripture we will become more and more aware of God. We will see His love and wrath, His mercy and justice, acted out on the pages of these ancient texts. And we will know more and more about God's personal care for us and His desire for us to respond to Him.

We can expect to improve our relationships. Human nature is remarkably resilient; over the millenniums we have changed little. Scripture shows us brothers who hate each other enough to kill, and friends who love each other more than their own lives. It shows us the grief of death and the joy of birth. It shows us the celebration of marriage and the pain of marriage ended. It pictures overwhelming generosity and the grudging hunger of greed. It echoes our hopeless moans at life's futility and it shouts our hope for life beyond this life. As Scripture increases our understanding of each other, we can expect to see its fruit wherever we touch other people: at work, in friendships, at churches, in neighborhoods, in casual encounters with waitresses and store clerks, and in the most challenging of all relationships: our families.

We can expect to better understand ourselves. Scripture is an intensely personal book. True, we may read it for historical content, or for its quality literature, or for its insightful teachings. But if Scripture is to accomplish its true purpose, we must read its pages, open ourselves, and allow it to read our souls. Scripture will show us our faults: the jealous brother, the greedy employee, the pompous religious leader. But as we let Scripture do its work, we will grow more and more according to God's design: the forgiving parent, the faithful leader, the wise friend, the one who models the love of Jesus Christ. And we will find the empty, God-shaped hole inside being filled by Christ Himself. Even people who don't believe much of what the Bible says, who are turned off by sermons and essays, can appreciate the questions here that allow them to examine the biblical text for themselves, explore its potential meanings, and form personal conclusions about response.

TruthSeed is appropriate for small group discussion or for personal use. Its blend of academic, personal, and relational tasks make it ideal for cell groups, workplace study groups, neighborhood groups, school-based groups, Sunday school classes, retreats, and outreach groups. It is also for personal study, meditation, and growth.

Suggestions for Group Discussion

1. There's no need to be a Bible expert to participate in a TruthSeed discussion. You may find experts in your group, but there is plenty of room for non-experts as well. Since the discussion centers around a single passage, you will all participate on a similar level. And God can grow any of us.

2. Arrive on time — out of consideration for other group members. Bring your TruthSeed guide and a Bible.

3. Commit to regular attendance. Understanding of the Scripture and relationships within the group are cumulative. You and others will benefit most if you can count on each other to be there. If you must be absent, call your host or leader ahead of time.

4. Discussion is a shared responsibility. It blends talking and listening in even balance. If you are a born listener, act on your responsibility to share your insights by making the extra effort necessary. If you are a born talker, sharpen your listening skills by keeping track of the flow of conversation. If you discover that you are "on stage" more than the average person present, shorten your comments and use them to draw other people into the conversation.

5. Treat other group members with respect. You cannot possibly agree with every comment throughout the course of a discussion study. Disagreement is one way to help each other grow toward the truth. But express your disagreement in kind terms that reflect a genuine respect for the person.

6. Guard the privacy of people in your group. Since spiritual growth makes a deep impact on our personal lives, you will likely hear others speak of their private feelings and events. And you may want to speak some of your own private thoughts. Agree together that you will not divulge each other's stories.

7. Don't gossip. Many groups pray together for a variety of needy people. It's tempting to get specific about names and weaknesses in a way that invites more speculation than prayer. Don't do it. It's possible to pray for a person with very little inside information. God knows it anyway.

8. Be willing to discuss the application questions. Some people are content to keep a group study at a purely academic level, so they read the questions that invite personal response, and pass on with the quick instruction to "think about it." But if Scripture is to be more than a textbook of information, we must allow it to penetrate our lives. Members of a group can nurture each other toward spiritual growth as they discuss together its personal impact.

9. Take note of the follow-up assignments. Each TruthSeed study ends with supplementary material that can provide further enrichment. In some cases, this section may prove as valuable as the rest of the study. So take advantage of this added resource.

10. Consider leading a discussion. Many groups rotate leadership so that almost everyone takes a turn asking the questions. This job does not require a lot of special skills, but a few pointers won't hurt. If it's your turn to lead, you will find notes for leaders beginning on page 71.

Suggestions for Personal Study

1. Settle into your favorite "quiet time" spot. Bring your Bible, the TruthSeed guide, writing materials, and (if you like) a commentary or Bible dictionary.

2. Pray. Ask God to reveal Himself to you as you study. Ask that He assist your understanding, that He bare your inner self to His gaze, and that He use your time to bring healing to your relationships.

3. Begin by reading the chapter introduction. Make notes about the first question and allow it to help you approach the topic you are about to study.

4. Read the assigned biblical text. If textual accuracy is one of your priorities, use a contemporary translation (not a paraphrase) that reflects recent scholarship. Mark significant words or phrases in your Bible, draw lines between ideas that seem connected, write questions or comments in the margins. Try reading aloud. It's one of the best ways to keep your mind from wandering.

5. Work through the list of questions. Jot notes in the space provided. Keep a journal of answers that require more space or more lengthy personal reflection.

6. Stop for periods of silence and meditation throughout your quiet time to allow God to work in your inner being.

7. Continue to pray as you study, asking God to reveal what He wants you to know of yourself and of Himself. Read aloud sections of the passage as a prayer inserting "I" and "me" where appropriate — or insert the name of someone you care about.

8. Don't feel that you must do an entire lesson at a single sitting. Feel free to break at natural division points or whenever you have "had enough" for now. Then come back on a different day, reread the text, review your work thus far, and pick up where you left off.

9. When you have completed your personal study of the questions, turn to the corresponding leader's notes in the back of the guide to gain further information you may have missed. If you are the studious type, refer to a commentary or Bible dictionary for more insights. The reading list at the end of the book provides a list of reliable resources.

10. Put into practice the follow-up activities at the end of each study. Read, sing, pray, do, meditate, journal, make the phone call, start the project, repair the relationship. When your study time is finished, God's work in your life has just begun. Allow His work to continue throughout the week.

As you use this TruthSeed guide, I pray that seeds of truth from God's Word will grow a rich harvest in your life.

—Carolyn Nystrom, Editor

Introducing Ephesians

Ephesians is no ordinary book. Begin reading it, and it's as if the veil between heaven and earth has been parted and we are being offered a heavenly perspective on what's happening here on earth.

All of Paul's other letters were written to put out certain fires in the church. But Ephesians is blissfully free of problems, presenting instead the glorious vision of God's plan for creation. It is a drama, the human drama, with talk of roles and parts and certain key players — including some good guys, some bad guys, and one particular arch enemy. Paul begins the plot with the Director — God, in conjunction with Jesus Christ and the Holy Spirit — at the beginning of time. Slowly, believers are cued to come on stage and instructed in how they should treat one another. Then unbelievers are added to the scene, and believers are told to guard their distinctiveness in order to fulfill their role in the world. Finally, the backdrop and props: Satan is trying his best to undermine God's work in and through believers, so believers must be aware of this fact and fight off his arrows with God's armor. Paul crafts his letter in a way that teaches his readers that human history begins with God and ends with God, and in between God works through His people (who live in a sin-filled world) to accomplish His purpose.

Paul wrote Ephesians from a prison in Rome, probably around A.D. 60–61. He had been arrested for preaching the Gospel. Scholars are not sure who Paul had in mind when he wrote Ephesians. It seems he didn't know his readers personally but had "heard about" their faith. This would explain his less personal tone (as compared with his letters to the Galatians or Corinthians, where he had firsthand knowledge of them and their situations), as well as the fact that our earliest manuscripts do not include the words "in Ephesus." Many scholars believe Ephesians was meant to be circulated to churches throughout Asia Minor by couriers like Tychicus (6:21-22). One possible explanation for how our translations came to contain the words "in Ephesus" is that Paul left a blank space in the introduction to be filled in by the messenger when he delivered it to a particular church. Though this theory has its problems, it seems to be the most plausible.

This study looks at Ephesians over 12 sessions, each session covering about half a chapter. The first session looks at the entire letter, to get an overview of the characters and plot. Each successive session then builds on the previous ones. If you are using this study as part of your regular small group meeting, or if you are using it on your own, optional suggestions are provided for group and personal response at the end of each session.

In my mind, the message of Ephesians ranks up there with that of Genesis 1–3 and the book of Job: we want to know where we come from (Genesis 1–3), and why suffering is such a part of our lives (Job), and we also need to know the radical difference Christ makes in our lives (Ephesians), and how that difference affects our relationships with other Christians and with unbelievers.

I hope you will grasp the heavenly perspective Paul gives us in Ephesians. Through faith in Christ we have become God's children, and each of us now has a part to play in His church. May we all, together, take our cues from the Heavenly Director.

Patti Picardi
1995

1
The Big Picture

Ephesians 1-6

We've all had experiences where we realize the importance of context. You walk into a meeting after it has started and don't understand what people are discussing, or you doze off in class and later try to enter into the discussion by asking an intelligent sounding question only to find it was voiced earlier — while you were dozing, no doubt. It's hard to come in on the middle of something and know what is going on.

In a way that is what we are up against when we try to understand a book like Ephesians. Certain things were going on at the time Paul wrote his letter, some of which he specifically mentions and others we must try to infer from what he says. The problem is complicated by the fact that a lot of time has passed since Paul wrote this letter, and some of the concerns the church faced then are not our concerns, while some of the issues that we would like God to speak to were not issues back then. When we read Ephesians we are entering into a "discussion" that had already begun between Paul and the churches for which he was responsible. We need to understand that context so that we can ask the right questions about what is being discussed.

That's why we begin our study of Ephesians by reading the whole book. Ephesians is what is called an *epistle,* and epistles are like letters. They were written for a specific reason or occasion — scholars call them "occasional documents" — and their individual parts or verses were meant to be understood in the context of the whole letter. So we will first look at Paul's entire letter to the Christians in Asia Minor in order to understand his overall purpose, or occasion, for writing to them. This aerial view provides a framework from which we will zero in on the individual parts of Ephesians in future studies.

Having read the section *Introducing Ephesians*, let's now open the door and walk into Paul's conversation with these first-century believers.

1. What is your normal way of handling mail such as bills, advertisements, and solicitation letters?

   How do you respond differently when the mail is a letter from someone you deeply care about?

Read aloud Ephesians 1–6

2. As you read, assume that you are reading a letter from someone important to you. How do you think Paul's readers reacted when they received his letter?

3. What are some of the main subjects Paul addresses in this letter?

4. The "occasion" for Paul's writing to the Christians in Asia Minor is to remind them that the church includes both Jewish and Gentile believers; there are no cultural, racial, or social barriers in "the body of Christ." What are some verses that speak to this issue?

5. Even though very little is said about Paul's relationship to the recipients of his letter, what can we conclude from the tone of the letter and some specific statements Paul makes?

6. Ephesians can be divided into two main parts: chapters 1–3 and chapters 4–6. What titles would you give to these two sections and why?

7. Why do you think Paul constructed his message in these two sections?

8. Sometimes we try to be something we aren't. The basic message of Ephesians is: "This is who Christ has created you to be. Now *be* it." When have you tried to be something or someone you aren't? What was the result?

9. Think of a situation in your life where it would help to remember who Christ has created you to be. How do you imagine it would help?

Ephesians 4:24 says that we are to "put on the new self." How can you begin to put on the new self in the situation you described above?

10. What questions do you have after reading Ephesians all the way through? Make note of your questions and the references.

11. What is particularly encouraging to you about Paul's message? Why is this meaningful to you?

Group Response

Choose three or four hymns and/or praise songs that speak about who we are in Christ—the message of Ephesians. ("O for a Thousand Tongues to Sing" is one example.) If a member of the group plays an instrument, have him or her lead your singing; otherwise sing a cappella.

Personal Response

Begin this week to keep a journal of your thoughts, questions, and insights into the book of Ephesians. Write two or three goals that you would like to accomplish as you study this epistle. These goals might concern studying Scripture, praying more regularly, demonstrating the Christlike character mentioned in Ephesians in a specific situation or relationship, worshiping God in a deeper way, or keeping a journal as a way of life.

2
God's Plan
from the Beginning

Ephesians 1:1-14

Some people simply radiate with joy—as if they know some wonderful secret that transforms everything they are and do. Brother Lawrence was like that. He cultivated his heart and mind to know God by reflecting on images he saw in Scripture, or people, or nature, that reminded him of who he was in Christ.

In *The Practice of the Presence of God*, Brother Lawrence tells the story of how at eighteen he saw a barren tree in the dead of winter. Its leaves were gone, giving it the appearance of death. But then he was reminded of how the spring would bring new life and color to this tree, and it would bear fruit. The image of God's power and care over all things—including him—was thereafter indelibly etched in Brother Lawrence's mind. It was the "secret" that permeated everything he was and did.

Paul was another who deeply appreciated what God had done for him in Christ—and it showed. From reading Ephesians we get the sense that he was saturated with the knowledge of God's love and forgiveness and purpose for his life. That reality transformed how he viewed everything, his joys as well as his sufferings—and he suffered greatly for the sake of Christ. But the source of his joy was no secret. He longed for all believers to know what he knew, using rich imagery to help his readers appreciate the life they had in Christ.

Are we so different from Brother Lawrence or Paul? Was their experience of God truly exceptional, or can we too know the "secret"? As you read these opening verses of Ephesians, let your soul, mind, and heart steep for a while in the marvelous and mysterious truths Paul proclaims. They can change the way you view life too.

1. Suppose you are preparing to make a speech. The person introducing you to the audience asks you to write three items of information that describe who you are. What do you write?

   Suppose you want someone to know you on a more personal level—what made you the person you are today. What events from your life do you want that person to know?

   Read aloud Ephesians 1:1-14

2. In what ways does Paul describe those who are "in Christ"?

   How is this different from the way we typically think of ourselves?

3. Of all these "spiritual blessings," which one do you think you appreciate the most? The least? Explain your answer.

4. Paul often blessed his readers with grace and peace—as he does
   in verse 2. "Grace" is a derivative of the typical Greek greeting,
   and "peace" *(shalom)* was the standard Jewish greeting. Based
   on your knowledge of the people in Paul's audience and their
   situation, why do you think he did this?

5. Paul speaks in verse 9 of the mystery of God's will. In view of
   the rest of the text, what is this mystery?

   In what sense is God's will (as it is described here) a mystery?

6. Paul locates the salvation of believers between, on the one
   hand, the fact that God had their salvation in mind from the
   beginning (verse 4) and, on the other hand, the fact that God
   will one day bring all creation under His rule (verse 10). What
   are some possible responses to God's foreknowledge and the
   certainty of His plan?

   What seems to be Paul's response to God having this kind of
   power and knowledge? What verses support your answer?

7. Where do you think most people believe the world is headed?

   What might their response be to the news that God is in control of human history and one day all creation will bow before Him?

8. If a family member or friend were asked how your life demonstrated an understanding of God's overall plan, what do you hope they would say?

9. Paul uses words like "predestined," "chosen," "God's plan," and "will" to describe the salvation of believers. What do these words imply about our part and God's part in our eternal destiny?

10. Paul says in verses 13-14 that those who are in Christ are "marked" (NASB uses "sealed") with the Holy Spirit as an assurance that they are God's people. What practical benefit can this assurance have for you and for the body of Christ as a whole?

Group Response

People who are marked by God's Spirit live in a different way than they would otherwise. Galatians 5:22-23 lists the nine-fold "fruit of the Spirit." Read this passage, then choose an evidence of the Spirit that you desire to exhibit more. There may be a certain relationship or situation that is particularly challenging for you right now, and this mark can bring restoration and healing. Pair up in twos to share these hopes. Then agree to pray for your partner throughout the week that this specific fruit might be borne in his or her life.

If time is short, jot your name and a brief description of how you hope to exhibit one particular fruit of the Spirit as you deal with a particular situation this week. Then exchange papers with others in the group and pray each day for the person whose name you receive.

Close your time together by prayerfully singing about your intentions. Suggested song: "In My Life, Lord, Be Glorified."

Personal Response

This week write in your journal some of your thoughts and questions concerning the topic of predestination. What implications of this truth are difficult for you to grapple with? Ask the Holy Spirit to give you understanding into your questions.

3
Thanks
and Praise

Ephesians 1:15-23

Over the years I've thought about the concept of "planned obsolescence" and balked at its philosophy. Even if you've never heard of the concept you've bought into it — literally. Disposable razors that stay sharp for only a few shaves, contact lenses you wear for a week and throw away, cameras that work for one roll of film — planned obsolescence has become a fundamental aspect of our economy. Even when we *try* to build things to last they eventually wear out, break, or become unsafe to use. "New is better."

As a New Englander, and a lover of tradition, I could let this depress me. It struck me recently, however, that maybe the fact that nothing lasts forever could be cause for celebration. In a way, it causes me to long for the permanence of heaven. And the longer I live the more often I think about heaven. Maybe God built this frustration into the "system" for this very reason.

In many ways, the Gospel challenges this trend toward impermanence, a trend that affects not only the way we spend our money, but also how we treat relationships and what we think about God. For one thing, there is nothing "new" about God. God never changes, or wears out, or needs replacing. Also, God wants our faith to last — to weather the storms and actually become stronger with time.

Paul's prayer for his readers gives us the sense that we can always go deeper with God: more wise, understanding, loving, and obedient — like a tree planted by a stream that sends down roots deep into the earth and so becomes stable and fruitful. Paul also wants his readers to grasp the hope, the riches, and the power of God — because he knows what a difference these make in the way people live. One person builds on sand, another builds on rock, and only time will reveal which is which. Paul prays that they know the One who builds people that last.

1. Think about the people in your life for whom you feel a responsibility (children, elderly parents, spouse, friends). How and what do you pray for them?

Read aloud Ephesians 1:15-23

2. Paul, as an apostle of the church, had a strong sense of responsibility for the Christians in Asia Minor. What all does he pray for his readers?

3. Paul begins his prayer by saying that he never stops "giving thanks" for these Christians, but remembers to "keep asking" God to provide for them (verses 16-17). What can we infer from these passages about the nature of prayer and about our part in praying for others?

When have you prayed for someone regularly, and what did God teach you through it about God, yourself, or the person?

4. If you knew someone like Paul was praying for you (as the Ephesians did), what difference would it make in your life?

5. Faith is a supernatural process. Paul says in verses 17 and 18 that we need "the Spirit of wisdom and revelation" and that our hearts need to be "enlightened." What does this say about the spiritual condition of human beings, apart from Christ?

6. When Paul refers in verse 18 to "the hope to which He has called you" and "the riches of His glorious inheritance," what is he talking about?

Rev. 21 - powerful description of heaven

7. What do God's *hope* and *riches* mean to you?

Heaven on earth   vs.   Heaven in the skies

How do the hope and riches that Paul describes apply both to the present and to the future?

Oct. 25/98

8. Paul reminds his readers in verses 19 and 20 that they possess the same kind of power as that which raised Christ from the dead! Give examples of how you see this power being worked out in your life.

9. Study verses 20-23. How would you describe the picture Paul paints here of Christ and His supreme authority?

10. Because of the authority that Christ possesses, Paul describes Him as the "head" of the church, and the church (us) as His "body" (verses 22-23). What is Paul trying to communicate with these images?

11. What relationship in your life would benefit from remembering that Christ possesses authority over all human and spiritual powers?

How do you think conflicts that arise in your church would be helped by remembering the unity that we have with Christ and with one another through Christ?

Group Response

Spend time together giving thanks and praise to God for all He has given us in Christ. Thank Him both for what He has done for the church as His body and for what He has done for the members of your group. Pray for the needs and concerns mentioned in question 11. End your time together by singing the Doxology.

Doxology
Praise God from whom all blessings flow,
Praise Him all creatures here below,
Praise Him above ye heavenly host,
Praise Father, Son, and Holy Ghost.
Amen.

Personal Response

✦ Read back over Ephesians 1. What does Paul tell you that God has done on your behalf?

✦ What are you particularly grateful for?

✦ Record your thoughts in your journal, and let these realities shape how you pray this week.

4
We're Either Alive or Dead

Ephesians 2:1-10

I t's difficult to describe what it looks like when God makes
something "alive," but I'll try. When I was about fourteen I had
an experience of doubting God's existence that shook me to the
core. It was summer, and I was in sailing camp in Old Greenwich,
Connecticut.

Every morning I rode my bike down to the beach, trying to arrive
early enough to pray and read Scripture before camp started. A
small garden near the camp was the perfect setting for reflection.
Someone tended this little sanctuary so that a variety of plants,
trees, flowers, animals, and birds could flourish there.

This particular morning I arrived before the sun had made its way
over the surrounding hedge of trees. All was silent and dark in the
garden. With my back to the garden I sat looking out over Long
Island Sound, watching the day begin and reflecting. Like someone
who barges into a private discussion, it seemed as if Satan whispered
to me in the middle of my thoughts: "You fool. Who are you
praying to? God doesn't really exist; He's just part of your imagina-
tion, your longing. This faith of yours may make you a better
person in this life, but you'll find there's nothing and no one wait-
ing for you in the next." He left me and I was paralyzed in my
thoughts.

The universe seemed to be having a grand, perverse laugh at my
expense. Everyone but me knew the truth: God didn't exist. The

only thing that was real was what I could see and touch. In the amount of time it takes to change your mind my view of reality was dismantled. I wanted to die.

That was when I turned to face the garden. I turned just as the sun rose over the evergreens and maples to touch the garden with light. What had been a picture of stillness and potential in shadowy grays was instantly transformed. The colors, the sounds, the smells — *life* was everywhere. Flower faces met the sun's gaze straight on; birds and rabbits and squirrels moved out from the shadows and into the warm light; earth and grass exhaled their breath. I knew what it meant, and I was restored by its message.

Satan had challenged my belief with a whisper. Now it was as if God took my face in His hands and said to me gently but with finality, "You cannot experience my creation — that I make alive — and say that I don't exist."

Listening to Satan makes a person dead; God's touch makes a person alive. I know what that looks like, and I'll never forget.

1. Describe a time when you felt especially "alive." What were some of the reasons why you felt that way?

Read aloud Ephesians 2:1-10

2. In this passage, Paul uses words like *alive* and *dead* to describe people's relationship to God. What phrases does Paul use in verses 1-3 to describe a person without Christ?

How would you sum up these phrases?

3. Look at verses 3-5. Even though they are now "in Christ," Paul reminds his readers that this was not always so. God showed them mercy when they were still sinners. Why do you think this would be important for them to remember?

   Who in your life needs your mercy—even though they don't deserve it?

4. In verse 3, Paul says that once they were "by nature objects of wrath." What do you think he means by this seemingly harsh language?

5. Verse 7 speaks of "the incomparable riches of His grace." In view of verses 5-7, how does our salvation—or anyone's—demonstrate the extraordinary measure of God's grace?

6. The message that we are saved by grace and not by what we do runs contrary to everything in our nature and our culture. What are some messages you hear, on the TV, radio, the movies, and magazines that say we can earn (and even deserve!) good things?

7. Which message do you think people get when they look at your life: "I am what God has made me by His grace" or "I've worked hard to get where I am"? Explain your answer.

8. Paul notes in verses 9-10 how, on the one hand, we are saved by grace and not works, and yet, on the other hand, we are saved in order to do good works. Why are both points important?

9. What are some of the good works you believe that God has "prepared" for you to do?

10. Sometimes the works God leads us to do involve great sacrifice, perseverance, and suffering. (Perhaps one of your answers to question 9 comes to mind.) Since God planned for you to do these good works, how can this knowledge motivate or encourage you to be faithful when times get hard?

Group Response

Keeping in mind people's answers to questions 9 and 10, commit to God the good works each person mentioned. Ask God to grant each one the wisdom to draw upon God's grace for which He has

made you "alive." End your time by singing with gratitude the
hymn "And Can It Be that I Should Gain."

Personal Response

◆ Set aside some time this week to reflect on your relationship
  with God. In what areas do you feel "alive" to God?

◆ Where do you sense God's Spirit putting to death old habits?

◆ Write your thoughts in your journal.

5
We Are
One in the Spirit

Ephesians 2:11-22

Some days I may *feel* far from God, but when Paul described the Gentiles as "far" from God it was no feeling — they really *were.* Some background information may be helpful to understand what he meant.

God had a special relationship with the Jews. He promised to protect and prosper them, and they in turn were to keep His laws. These laws, which included specific animal sacrifices and purity rituals, kept the Jews separate and distinct from all other nations. The same laws also prevented Gentiles from having access to God, since a person's righteousness was judged by how well he fulfilled the law's requirements. But in God's mind there was always a greater purpose for cultivating this special relationship with the Jews. These people and their laws were to be examples of God's grace and mercy, not his favoritism. They were a bridge built to get to Christ.

The sacrifice Christ made on the cross accomplished what animal sacrifices never could: forgiveness of sins. Because of Jesus, those whom the law temporarily barred now could be joined together with the law keepers to create one new people. This was a radical message, and one which perhaps required more of an adjustment for the Jews than the Gentiles (sometimes it's easier to move up the ladder than down). *The New Bible Commentary*'s introduction to Ephesians describes the situation this way:

If we imagine a situation in the New Testament period of church history when the Gentile mission had prospered and Gentiles were streaming into the church—when they were boasting of their supposed independence of Israel, and were becoming intolerant of their Jewish Christian brethren—then we have a life-setting which makes the epistle understandable in the Pauline literature.

In this passage Paul challenges the attitudes of both Jewish and Gentile believers. He declares the oneness of all believers in Christ, while reminding his Gentile readers that they were not always part of the "in" crowd.

1. When have you felt excluded from the "in" crowd? Describe the situation and how it made you feel.

unification of the Jews & Gentiles

Read aloud Ephesians 2:11-22

2. The Gentiles were once excluded from God's promises, but now, in Christ, God has made a new people by bringing together Jews and Gentiles. In the space below, list what Paul says used to be true about his readers before they knew Christ and what is now true because of their relationship with Christ. Include the corresponding verse references.

Before	*After*

3. The "covenants of the promise" mentioned in verse 12 refers to God's promise to give the Israelites land, descendants, and a unique relationship with God—which helps explain why Paul said in verse 12 that the Gentiles were "without hope and with-

out God in the world." How have the Gentiles now been brought near because of Christ?

4. Verse 14 says that a "wall of hostility" separated Jews from Gentiles. How does verse 15 help to explain that separation?

5. We have no true equivalents to the kind of barrier to salvation that existed between Jews and Gentiles. We do, however, erect other types of barriers within the church. What are some "walls" that Christians put up that could exclude people from salvation?

6. From verses 14-18, what does Paul say Christ has accomplished by His death and resurrection?

7. The body of Christ is made up of all kinds of people, because a person's race, culture, or class makes no difference to Him. Using Paul's metaphor of the body (verse 16), describe what happens to Christ's body when Christians try to discriminate against fellow Christians.

8. The relationship between Christ's death and "the Law" has long been a subject of debate among Christians. In view of this passage, how would you explain how Christ's death on the cross has abolished the Law.

9. Verses 19-22 speak to the full inclusion ("fellow citizens") of the Gentiles into the church. Instead of the temple, Jewish and Gentile believers now become God's dwelling place. What implications do these verses have for Gentile believers, Jewish believers, and the church that unites both?

10. How could you better express your own unity with other Christian believers?

Group Response

✦ Spend some time praying for the church, that it would repent of the ways that it sets up barriers to people coming to faith, and that it would faithfully proclaim and demonstrate only Christ's conditions for faith.

✦ Pray for each church represented in your group.

✦ Pray (by name) for one or more leaders in your own church.

✦ End by praying the Lord's Prayer.

Personal Response

Based on what you learned in this study, pray for God's direction as you choose one attitude toward other believers that needs to change. Make a list of specific ways you can be more like Christ in this area, then look for opportunities this week to put them into practice.

6
Paul's Prayer for the Church

Ephesians 3:1-21

S ome of the most meaningful prayers I have heard have been offered by my friends. Knowing who they are, why they pray as they do, and how God has touched them personally helps me to appreciate what they pray.

I wonder what the Ephesians knew about Paul. When he prayed for them in this letter could they hear his experience of God coming through? They must have known that, at one time, Paul had been a Pharisee, a strict observer of the Jewish law. Word had probably also spread that this Pharisee used to go to great lengths to prevent the Gospel from spreading. But did they know about how, one day when Paul was headed for Damascus to chase down some Christians, Jesus Christ actually appeared to him and convinced him of His identity? What about the five times Paul was flogged, the three times he was beaten, the time he was stoned, the shipwrecks, hunger, and constant danger he endured—all to preach the Gospel? Did they appreciate how these experiences shaped his prayers?

In the third chapter of Ephesians we see Paul marveling at how he, one of the staunchest enemies of the faith, became the one to whom God chose to reveal His plan for human history—and the part the church plays in fulfilling that plan. Paul could call himself, "less than the least of all God's people" because he knew the "unsearchable riches of Christ" about which he was commissioned to preach.

Paul tells his readers that they too have a role to fulfill together as members of Christ's body. As you read about Paul's revelation and his prayer for the church, ask yourself: Who was Paul? What is God's purpose for the church? And how is God at work in human history?

1. If you knew that someone you loved was suffering so that you would be better off, what do you think your reaction would be?

Read aloud Ephesians 3:1-21

2. Paul mentions his suffering in verses 1 and 13. What all does he say to explain why he is suffering?

3. Paul was a prisoner in Rome when he wrote Ephesians, yet in verse 1 he calls himself a "prisoner of Christ Jesus." What is he saying by making this distinction?

Why might this distinction be important to Paul and also to his readers?

4. Most of us have not suffered imprisonment because of doing what is right — though some have. But most of us have suffered

smaller hurts and losses. When have you suffered for doing what was right?

What were some of your reactions to your suffering then, and how has your perspective changed with the benefit of hindsight?

5. Focus on verses 3-6. Paul writes that the mystery revealed in Christ is that Jews *and* Gentiles may draw near to God by faith. Why do you suppose God chose to work progressively through history, first with the Jews and then through them to all people groups, instead of revealing Himself all at once?

6. Paul often encourages his readers to understand the "big picture" of God at work in history, in order to interpret His specific work in their lives. Here Paul talks about the role of the church by noting its place in history. According to verses 10-11, what is God's purpose for the church?

What are some ways in which your local church is fulfilling this purpose?

7. In verses 14-19, how does Paul pray for his readers and what does he pray for them?

8. How can we *know* a love that "surpasses knowledge"? (verse 19)

9. Some people take verse 20 to mean that we can ask God for anything we want and He will give it to us. In view of your discussion of question 8, how would you respond to this interpretation?

10. How do verses 20 and 21 sum up all that Paul has written so far?

11. God desires that both Jews and Gentiles follow Him, and that they would always grow deeper in the love of Christ. Paul's prayer in verses 16-21 is that the church may grasp these facts. What part of his prayer is particularly meaningful to you?

What step can you take this week to meditate on the truth of this aspect of knowing God?

Group Response

✦ Spend time praising God as the Creator, Sustainer, and Redeemer of the world, the One who has chosen to work through human history, becoming one of us so that we could know Him.

✦ End your time by singing a hymn like "Crown Him with Many Crowns" or "All Hail the Power of Jesus' Name."

Personal Response

Take time this week to research how God has worked progressively in human history. Two good sources of information are the *Evangelical Dictionary of Theology* (Walter A. Elwell, editor, 1984) and the *International Standard Bible Encyclopedia* (Geoffrey W. Bromiley, editor, 1982). Look up the topic of "covenant" to learn about how God has worked progressively in human history in the lives of people like Noah, Abraham, Moses, David, and finally Jesus, to reveal Himself to the world.

7
United
We Stand

Ephesians 4:1-16

My volleyball coach in high school would get excited when we played as a team — not as a bunch of individuals. He used all sorts of images to describe the oneness we would achieve (temporarily) on the court as well as our more frequent chaos. On a good day he said our defense was like fluid that filled every crevice of the court. On a bad day when our spikes lacked a coherent strategy, we were more like random notes strung together but making no music. When he gave us these pep talks about playing "our game" we knew he wasn't asking each of us to play exactly like every other player. We were to play in a way that allowed our individual strengths to come forth — for the benefit of the whole team. He'd shout, "You know the rules, you have the skills, you've practiced the drills, you have what it takes to win — so get out there and play your game!"

Those memories help me picture how God wants each member of the body of Christ to play on His team. Paul uses all sorts of metaphors in Ephesians to describe what the church is because of Christ. The first half of his letter is a holy pep talk of who God's people are: holy, predestined, filled with the Spirit, under Christ's authority, alive, members of God's household, full of hope. What a picture! So when, in the second half of his letter, Paul exhorts his readers to "live a life worthy of the calling you have received," his instruction is based on all that he has just said about who they are.

God never requires anything of us that He doesn't equip us to do.

Paul is saying that because when we are "in Christ" we have the grace to live like the changed people we are.

1. Think of a time when you received a "pep talk." How did the person motivate you and why did it energize you?

Read aloud Ephesians 4:1-16

2. What qualities should characterize those who are called?

How do these characteristics promote unity among Christians?

3. By repeating the word "one" seven times in verses 4-6, Paul stresses how crucial it is for the church to be united. Describe the kind of unity that Paul is talking about.

Why is unity in the church so important?

4. Think of an experience you have had concerning unity in the church. How does it compare with the definition Paul gives for unity?

5. A better translation of verse 7 would be: "Grace has been given to each one according to the measure of Christ's gift." What three important elements does Paul teach in this verse and why are all three important?

6. Verses 8-10 are confusing. Some scholars understand the quote from Psalm 68 to be a reference to Pentecost and the coming of the Holy Spirit's gifts. Assuming that this is correct, what does Paul mean in verse 10 when he says that Christ has filled "the whole universe"?

7. In verse 11, Paul identifies five types of gifts that Christ gives to the church. These gifts come in the form of people, who serve the church for specific reasons. What are these people-gifts and why have they been given? (Study verses 12-13.)

8. Verses 12-14 speak of spiritual maturity as a goal. How then should we respond to spiritual infancy in the church?

   How do you need to be more spiritually mature? Try to be specific.

9. In verses 14-16, Paul says that Christians do not remain spiritual infants, but "maintain the truth" (a better translation of verse 15 than "speaking the truth") as they grow up in Christ together. Just as the many different parts of our own body function together as a whole unit, so Christians are called to be united for the sake of the Gospel. How does this passage challenge you to function in the church in a more united way?

   What can you do to begin exercising this insight in your own church?

Group Response

Sum up your discussion on unity by singing the hymn "The Church's One Foundation."

Personal Response

Do you know someone in your church who seems to operate on the fringes of church life? Maybe this individual just comes to worship on Sunday mornings and never has any other contact the rest of the week. How can you share what you have learned about the unity of the church in a way that would encourage this person to see himself or herself as a necessary part of the body of Christ?

8
Created to Be Like God

Ephesians 4:17-32

Sometimes I am keenly aware of the power of my words. In some small way they seem to either build people up or tear them down, further their growth in godliness or more firmly resolve them in their sin. And it's not just my words that have this power—so do my actions.

C. S. Lewis made an observation along these lines in his essay *The Weight of Glory*. While some may not agree with everything he says here, I think we must give thoughtful pause to his idea that the way we treat one another has eternal importance.

> It may be possible for each to think too much of his own potential glory hereafter; it is hardly possible for him to think too often or too deeply about that of his neighbour. The load, or weight, or burden of my neighbour's glory should be laid daily on my back, a load so heavy that only humility can carry it, and the backs of the proud will be broken. It is a serious thing to live in a society of possible gods and goddesses, to remember that the dullest and most uninteresting person you talk to may one day be a creature which, if you saw it now, you would be strongly tempted to worship, or else a horror and a corruption such as you now meet, if at all, only in a nightmare. All day long we are, in some degree, helping each other to one or the other of these destinations. It is in the light of these overwhelming possibilities, it is with the awe and the circumspection proper to them, that we should conduct all our dealings with one another, all friendships, all loves, all play, all politics. There are no ordinary

people . . . your neighbour is the holiest object presented to your senses.

Paul was deeply concerned that his readers promote the work of the Holy Spirit in each other and not return to familiar sinful habits. His concern was twofold: that their unity be preserved as well as their witness in a hostile and alien society. We have all felt the deadly effects of anger, gossip, crude jokes, or lies. Just as we protect our own bodies from harmful things, Christians, who are members of the same body, need to protect their body from behavior that would harm it. Letting go of old sinful habits takes work though, because sin is sometimes a lot more comfortable than holiness. Paul knew all about this struggle (Romans 7) and spoke to the heart of the matter.

1. We all have a favorite pair of old jeans or slippers or a hat that we put on when we want to be really comfortable. What is your favorite piece of old clothing, and what makes it so comfortable?

Read aloud Ephesians 4:17-32

2. Sometimes we put on our old sinful ways of behaving like a favorite piece of clothing. It's comfortable and familiar. How does Paul describe people who are controlled by their sinful desires?

How does he describe people who are controlled by the Spirit?

3. Since Christians have already been saved from their sin, so that it no longer controls them, why do we have to *keep* putting off our "old self"?

4. Putting off the old self is only one half of the picture. Paul says in verse 24 that we must also put *on* the new self. Why is this second step necessary?

5. Think of a time when you had to put off your old self and put on your new one. What was the situation and what did you learn about either the nature of sin or the power of God?

6. Imagine that, in the situation you just described, an unbeliever observed you choosing to "put off" and "put on." He or she wants to know why. How do you explain your decision in a way that is understandable *and* winsome to this person?

7. Paul contrasts the futility of the *world's* way of *thinking* with the renewing quality of *godly thinking*. (Compare verse 17 with verses 23-24.) Why do you think Paul locates both depravity and rejuvenation in the *mind*?

8. You may have heard this statement: Right thinking produces right conduct. How have you seen this expression lived out in your life?

9. Study verses 25-32. How does Paul exhort his readers to live lives that are radically different from those around them?

    Do Not   *Do*

    What do the "do nots" have in common?

    How are the "dos" similar?

10. Which of the "do nots" is most difficult for you to avoid?

    What is one way you can put on the new self in this area?

Group Response

✦ Pray for one another that each would desire to please God more than themselves.

✦ Ask God to continue to show each one who they are in Christ as well as how their choices, the good and the bad, affect the well being of the body of Christ.

✦ End with the Lord's Prayer.

Personal Response

Choose a mature Christian friend and ask that person to pray for you in the area you mentioned in question 10 and to periodically ask you how you are doing in this area.

9
Light in the Darkness

Ephesians 5:1-20

Light versus darkness is a common theme in Scripture. In the beginning God made light to separate out the darkness. The psalmist called Scripture "a light for my path." Jesus referred to Himself as the "light of the world." Jesus said that His disciples were light too, and that they were not to hide their light but to illumine the darkness around them. Throughout the Bible, we see light characterizing God's work in the world.

In a sense darkness hates light, since darkness cannot exist in the presence of light. The very nature and essence of light is to illumine, to expose, to make clear or visible what was not. Light overpowers darkness. What an illustration of God's power over sin and Satan! And what a helpful reminder, when our culture (and some Christians) become overly preoccupied with Satan's schemes.

God's purpose for the church is to be light in a dark world. Paul tells his readers to live as children of light. In this section of his letter, Paul begins a new application of what it means to be "in Christ." In previous sections, he wrote about its meaning for them personally and how they are therefore to treat one another. Now he discusses its implications for how they are to live in the midst of an alien and hostile world.

1. When children are little they learn a lot from mimicking their parents. Give some examples of how you have seen children

imitate. (How do you remember imitating someone older than you?)

Read aloud Ephesians 5:1-20

2. Verse 1 begins with the command, "Be imitators of God." What phrases can you find throughout this passage that show what an imitator of God does and is?

3. Focus on verses 1-7. How would you describe the contrast between children of light and children of darkness?

4. Give one example of how you are trying to imitate God in your day-to-day situations.

Where are you tempted to conform in a wrong way to your surroundings rather than be God's light?

5. Verse 8 tells us that we are to "live as children of light." What all does Paul mean by this statement?

6. Verse 11 says that believers are to expose the darkness. How?

How do unbelievers react in your presence?

7. Today it is considered acceptable — even healthy — to talk about all our deepest sins and desires. Instead of confiding in ministers or priests, people "confess" (or brag) to talk show hosts. Why do you think Paul warned believers against such behavior? (See verse 12.)

8. In essence, Paul's cautions in verses 15-20 can be grouped into three areas: our thoughts, deeds, and words. What does he suggest that we do to keep ourselves pure in each of these areas?

Thoughts:

Deeds:

Words:

9. This passage says in verse 18 that we are to be "filled with the Spirit" while verse 10 reminds us to "find out what pleases the

Lord." In what area of your life do you sense the Holy Spirit prompting you to find out what pleases the Lord?

10. Make a list of the opportunities you currently have to shine the light of Christ into this dark world.

What step can you take this week (perhaps together with other believers) to allow God's light in you to expose this darkness?

Group Response

✦ Take time to pray along the lines of your discussion. Pray for the collective witness of the church around the world, that it will be faithful to exercise its role as light to the world.

✦ Pray for the witness of your local congregation, that unbelievers in your community will be compelled by your example of integrity and love.

✦ Pray for the personal example of the members of your group, that each would find out what pleases the Lord in the circumstances of their lives.

✦ Close your time by praying the Lord's Prayer.

Personal Response

Set aside a chunk of time (a morning, a day) this week to be still before the Lord. Ask the Holy Spirit to shine His light on any areas of sexual immorality, impurity, or greed in your life. Record your thoughts in your journal. Confess your need for God's Spirit to strengthen you in this area, and ask a mature Christian to periodically ask you how you are doing in this area of weakness.

10

As unto the Lord

Ephesians 5:21-33

A dam recognized a profound mystery when he said to Eve, "This is now bone of my bones and flesh of my flesh." By design, marriage affords the greatest potential for intimacy, encouragement, and companionship—when the focus is right. When the focus is wrong, however, the potential for heartbreak and suffering is equally great. In an age where self-fulfillment is the primary criteria by which we judge our commitments, the challenge for believers is to allow the Bible to inform our understanding of marriage and not our culture or experience.

The Bible speaks about different aspects of marriage in several places; some texts discuss marriage and divorce, others address marriage between believers and unbelievers, and still others expound the benefits of remaining single. No one passage is comprehensive, but each one sheds more light on what marriage is and is not.

Paul's teachings in Ephesians adds one of those dimensions to the meaning of marriage. Along the lines of his general theme of being united in Christ, Paul now says that the oneness between husbands and wives in some ways reflects the unity between God and the church. When a husband and wife express their love and submission to each other they are imaging what is true between Christ and the church. As Paul said, "This mystery is great."

1. Under what conditions are you most inclined to give to some-

one sacrificially and selflessly? Explain.

Note: When Paul wrote his instructions to husbands and wives he assumed the context of a loving, Christ-centered relationship. (Paul gives instructions concerning marriage to unbelievers elsewhere.)

Read aloud Ephesians 5:21-33

2. What does Paul say is the reason for submitting and loving in marriage?

Why is this foundation so important?

3. In verse 22, Paul tells wives to submit to their husbands as to the Lord. Based on your study of Ephesians so far, how would you describe the term "submission"?

What are some examples of the misuse of submission?

4. In verse 25, Paul tells husbands to love their wives as Christ loved the church. What are some ways husbands can love their wives in this way?

5. If you are married, what is one practical way that you can better practice submission and love out of reverence for Christ?

6. Paul relates this love and submission to the relationship already established with Christ. If you are a single person, how can you grow in love and submission to Christ?

7. What do you find difficult about these instructions to wives and husbands?

8. After Adam and Eve disobeyed God's instruction in the garden, God pronounced individual curses on them: the husband would now rule over his wife and the wife's desire would be for her husband (Genesis 3:16). How might these curses relate to the need for Paul's instruction?

9. In verses 31-33, Paul takes the "one flesh" statement of Genesis 2:24 and applies it to the union between Christ and the church; the church is one with Christ. Based on your study of Ephesians so far, why do you think Paul compares the marriage relationship to the relationship between Christ and the church?

10. What insight have you gained from this study about the relationship between husbands and wives?

What insights have you gained about the relationship between Christ and the church?

What effect could your insights have on your own relationship with Christ?

Group Response

✦ Pray for one another about the concerns expressed during your discussion.

✦ Ask God to help each one see his or her status (single or married) as an opportunity in which to serve Christ.

✦ End your time with the Lord's Prayer.

Personal Response

This week do a Bible study on the passages in the New Testament that deal with the topic of marriage. Some examples are:

✦ Matthew 22:23-30

✦ Romans 7:1-3

✦ 1 Corinthians 7:1-16

✦ Hebrews 13:4

What is the central teaching of each passage? Record your insights in your journal.

11
Children and Parents/ Slaves and Masters

Ephesians 6:1-9

If you want to know the real me, there are two places to look: my family and my coworkers. These are the relationships in which I am most able to shine but also where I am most likely to fall.

It seems that Paul knew something about this tendency. Having just written to wives and husbands about how they are to submit to Christ in their relationships with each other, Paul now addresses children and their parents — along with slaves and their masters. As we read his instruction to slaves and masters, however, we need to be aware of a significant cultural difference between the first-century Roman Empire and today: slavery was a legally established part of first-century society. Comparing twenty-first-century democracy to first-century monarchy is in some ways like comparing apples and oranges: they are both fruits, but . . .

Because of these differences, the question of how to apply these teachings is not obvious. As Stuart and Fee discuss in *How to Read the Bible for All It's Worth*, our cultures do not share comparable situations, so this passage gives us an opportunity to practice one of the interpretive principles that is unique to literature like epistles. Epistles are letters written for a *specific occasion*. Just as you or I assume, when we write a letter, that our reader knows certain background information, Paul assumed that his readers knew the social structures of their day. Our first step then is to try to reconstruct the historical setting that Paul was addressing. From this, we can discern the principles on which he based his instruction. Only then can we make appropriate adjustments as we try to apply these principles in our own culture. (If you want to research these kinds of historical issues, you will find that Bible commentaries, encyclopedias, and dictionaries are helpful resources.)

But back to our own setting. To our modern democratic way of thinking we may wonder why Paul didn't sound a radical call for the overthrow of slavery (not to mention a less authoritarian view of parental responsibility). But if that is our primary concern, we miss what was truly radical about Paul's teaching. In fact, what was radical then is still radical. Paul's instructions to children and parents and to slaves and masters contain timeless teaching for Christians of all generations. We don't want to miss them.

1. How would you describe your relationship with your parents?

Read aloud Ephesians 6:1-9

2. How does this passage continue the theme of mutual submission that Paul began in 5:21?

3. What advice does Paul give to children and parents?

Does obeying and honoring our parents mean we are to do whatever they say? Explain.

4. How has your relationship with your parents changed as you've grown older?

   What are some ways that you can show honor to your parents now?

5. We know from other passages in Scripture that mothers are also to be involved in the training and discipline of children. Why then do you think that here Paul addressed only the fathers' responsibility for their children?

6. How does Paul's teaching here compare with your experience either as a parent or as a child growing up?

   What are some practical ways that parents can raise their children in the training and instruction of the Lord?

7. Look more carefully at verses 5-9. What specific instructions do you see for the way slaves and masters were to treat each other?

What reason does Paul give for masters and slaves to treat each other in this way?

8. What differences and what similarities do you see between the situation Paul was addressing and your own?

9. What timeless principles undergird Paul's specific instructions taught in this passage?

10. How could the principle of doing everything "as to the Lord" affect your work? (Your work may be raising children, studying for a degree, managing a business or a home, or whatever else fills most of your time.)

Group Response

✦ Pray for one another along the lines of what people mentioned in question 10.

✦ End by singing the hymn "May the Mind of Christ, My Savior."

Personal Response

Take time this week to consider your perspective toward your work. Do you work as if you were serving the Lord? Record in your journal what your current perspective is—as well as areas where you believe God is prompting a change of attitude. Pray for opportunities to practice the attitude Paul teaches in Ephesians.

12 To Arms!

Ephesians 6:10-24

For all the hype Satan receives in today's movies and popular Christian books, Scripture tells us remarkably little about him. We know that he was originally created to be one of God's angels. Satan, however, was not content with angel status. He wanted to be God, and that desire utterly destroyed him. Now, instead of being surrounded by the other angelic hosts who praise and serve God, Satan connives with the angels who followed him, and together they instigate evil and exercise a certain amount of power over this world. Scripture's many names for Satan reveal the nature of his purpose: Deceiver, Father of Lies, Accuser, The Tempter, Adversary, Angel of the Abyss, Prince of This World, and The Evil One.

But there is much that Scripture does not explain to us about Satan. For example, I wonder how Satan got into the garden of Eden to begin with. And what about that interesting exchange between God and Satan over Job? I'm struck by Scripture's silence on these and other concerns of mine, and challenged by my responsibility to keep Scripture's (God's) silence and not try to answer for it.

Jesus told his disciples to be "as shrewd as snakes and as innocent as doves"—a difficult balance to maintain. Satan probably would like nothing better than for Christians to spend all their time trying to be either snakes or doves, since it is only in the balance that God is truly glorified. In his preface to *The Screwtape Letters*, C.S. Lewis said:

There are two equal and opposite errors into which our race can fall about the devils. One is to disbelieve in their existence. The other is to believe, and to feel an excessive and unhealthy interest in them. They themselves are equally pleased by both errors.

Why would Paul end his letter to the Ephesians, which began with images of our glorious calling, with talk of Satan and warfare? From the time sin first entered the world, Satan has known of his defeat. He consoles himself with one thought: he may succeed in bringing others down with him. Paul wants his readers to understand why they will meet resistance as they live out their faith. He wants to show us God's weapons for fighting this war.

1. What do you think of the idea that there are unseen spiritual forces which affect our lives? Describe your view.

Read aloud Ephesians 6:10-24

2. What does this passage teach us about Satan? Cite verse references.

3. Reread verses 10-13. What hope do you find here for coping with evil forces?

4. Study all of the armor mentioned in verses 14-17. How would you describe the meaning and purpose of each?

5. Glance through verses 10-18 again looking for action words. What do these words suggest about your part in coping with evil?

6. As you think through the protection God offers you in this closing section of Ephesians, what are you especially thankful for and why?

Take a few moments right now to thank God for these gifts.

7. In verses 18-20, Paul tells his readers to pray. How and why?

8. Why might Paul have felt a special need for their prayers? (See verses 19-20.)

9. Paul asks specifically for prayer that he proclaim the Gospel fearlessly. Why don't believers need to be afraid over the reality that Satan and his forces want to destroy their faith?

10. Reread the quote by C.S. Lewis in the introduction to this study. How do you personally balance the extremes of seeing the devil around every corner and denying that he ever affects you?

11. Study the final words of Paul's letter in verses 21-23. What do you find satisfying about this closing greeting?

12. The book of Ephesians has two sections. The first half describes God's great eternal plan. The second speaks of practical ways to live with that plan in view. Hence the title of this guide: *Living toward Eternity.* Page back through all of Paul's letter to the Christians in Ephesus. What do you find here that could help you live toward eternity?

Group Response

✦ Sing the hymn "A Mighty Fortress is Our God."

✦ Close your time with the Lord's Prayer.

Personal Response

Reread the book of Ephesians. Notice how Paul develops his theme of the unity and purpose of the church. If you chose to do the personal response in chapter 1, go back over the goals you set for yourself during your study of Ephesians. Record your progress in your journal.

Notes for Leaders

Preparation

Begin your preparation with prayer and personal study. Prepare to lead your particular lesson by following the ten steps under *Suggestions for Personal Study* beginning on page 7.

Study the biblical context of the passage under consideration. Research any questions likely to sidetrack your group.

Study the flow of questions. TruthSeed questions are designed to create a flow of discussion from beginning to end. Get comfortable with the potential directions of the study. Mark pacing notes so that the discussion will spread evenly over your allotted time. Most TruthSeed studies should last about an hour.

Read the leader's notes for your particular study beginning on page 74. Mark information that you may need during the course of the study in the blank spaces of your question list.

Plan time divisions. Your group time may include other ingredients such as refreshments, music, worship, sharing, and prayer. Block out time units so that your group is able to accomplish all that is scheduled. Many TruthSeed lessons make suggestions for these additional ingredients at the close of the Bible study section.

Acknowledge to yourself and to God that the group belongs to the people in it, not to you as a leader. TruthSeed is designed to facilitate a group discovery form of learning moderated by a discussion leader. Plan to lead with the group's welfare and interests in mind.

Pray for each group member by name.

Group Time

Begin on time. No apology necessary. The group has come to-gether for a particular purpose and has assigned you the job of leading it in the study.

If your group is meeting for the first time, survey together the guidelines for group discussion beginning on page 6. This will help each person to know what is expected and will get you off on a common footing.

Take appropriate note of the narrative introduction at the be-ginning of the study then ask the opening question. Encourage responses from each person. When everyone seems involved in the subject at hand, the group will be ready to enter the biblical text. Since the opening questions point toward the text but do not inter-act with it, always ask the opening question BEFORE reading the Scripture.

Read the assigned Scripture passage aloud. Or, ask several group members to read. Some people feel embarrassed about their reading skills, so don't make surprise assignments unless you are certain that they will be well received. Paragraph breaks in the text mark natural thought divisions, so always read by paragraphs, not by verses.

Conduct a discussion of the biblical text using the questions supplied. TruthSeed questions should promote multiple answers and group interaction. Allow time for several people to respond to each question and to each other. If the group does not seem to understand a particular question, rephrase it until it becomes clear, break it into smaller units, or give a brief summary and move on.

Give encouraging comments. If an answer is partially right, ac-knowledge that part. If an answer seems inappropriate, say some-thing like, "What verse led you to that conclusion?" or "What do some of the rest of you think?"

Don't be afraid of silence. Help group members to become com-fortable with the quiet by announcing a "thinking time." Then invite them to share their thoughtful responses to the question at hand. Learn a sensitivity to God that can come from occasional silence.

Pace the study. It is the leader's responsibility to be sure that you finish on time and that the group has adequate time to discuss later questions. Some questions will take longer than others, so create a flexible pace with one eye on the clock and the other on the interests of your group. Don't be afraid to redirect attention to the question list or the biblical text. Suggest that you may come back to some interesting topic after you have finished the study.

Involve everyone—more or less equally. Draw in quiet people by asking for nonthreatening opinion responses. Avoid direct eye contact with someone who talks a bit too much. If necessary, point out the shared responsibility for a successful discussion by reading item 4 on page 6.

Avoid over-talking yourself. Groups with an overactive leader get tempted to sit back and let the leader do *all* the work. Eventually, this causes people to lose the benefit of a personal encounter with the Scripture as it impacts their own lives.

Keep the discussion on track. Consider writing the purpose statement from the leader's section at the top of your question page so that you can keep the discussion objective in mind. You can head off a tangent by gently directing attention back to the biblical text. But do consider the relative merit of any potential tangent. Sometimes apparent tangents represent real needs that the group ought to address. In that case, adjust your plan (for the moment) and follow the needs of the group. If the tangent seems of limited interest or importance, offer to talk about it in more detail at a later time. Or if the tangent is of great importance, but requires further preparation, ask the group to table it for this session, but come back to it at a later meeting.

Don't skip questions of personal application. Here is where Scripture does its most important work. As other group members respond, be ready to add your own experiences of God's work in your life.

Open and close your study with prayer. Or ask someone in your group to do so.

Study One
The Big Picture
Ephesians 1–6

Purpose: To practice the crucial interpretive principle of understanding Bible verses in their context by reading Paul's entire letter to the Christians in Asia Minor.

Question 1. Try to involve each person in responding to these questions. When we read a letter from a friend we picture the person writing us, and there is a sense of "this affects my life." We might be excited to hear their news, curious about what's inside, joyful that the person has written us, concerned about how the person is. As you direct the discussion, you might want to refer to how we read a love letter versus the newspaper: we pore over every word of a love letter, reading from beginning to end and then in-between the lines, but we skim the newspaper. Keep the responses in mind when discussing question 2.

Question 3. Allow time for people to thoughtfully page through Ephesians and point out themes and passages. Some examples are: new life in Christ (chapters 1 and 2), grace (2:4-5, 8-9), unity (2:11-22; 4:3-6), and submission (wives and husbands: 5:21-33; children and parents: 6:1-4; slaves and masters: 6:4-9).

Question 4. Your group might look at how Christ has reconciled the two groups by His work on the cross (2:11-18); how God chose to reveal His plan over time, first to the Jews and then through them to the world (3:2-6); and the "one Lord, one faith, one baptism, one God and Father of all" statement in 4:5-6. Allow people time to skim the letter for four or five examples.

Question 5. Paul does not know his recipients firsthand (1:15; 3:1-2); overall, he makes a less personal, more general appeal than in his other letters. (Recall from the introduction that Ephesians was probably meant to be circulated throughout Asia Minor and not for one specific group of people.) Paul has a special concern and sense of responsibility for these believers, as an apostle of Jesus Christ would. Encourage your group to find statements throughout the letter that imply tone or relationship. It will help the group "track" the comments if the person speaking gives verse references.

Question 7. Paul lays the foundation of who we *are* in Christ before addressing what we ought to *do*. It is a theme that is seen throughout Scripture: God's ethical commands are based on statements of fact. Truth and action cannot be separated. The mark of one who truly believes in the truth is right behavior. For examples, your group might point out, "There is one body and one Spirit" (4:4), "make every effort to keep the unity of the Spirit" (4:3), or because we are God's "holy people," "there must not be even a hint of sexual immorality" (5:3).

Question 8. Try to allow each person an opportunity to speak. Allow enough time for brief stories of personal experience. Be prepared to share one story about yourself.

Question 10. Allow for each person to raise a question or two. (Make notes for future reference.) Then ask that people bring up their questions again when you study the related passages.

Study Two
God's Plan from the Beginning
Ephesians 1:1-14

Purpose: To grow our understanding of who we are in Christ, which is grounded in an understanding of God's plan for all human history.

Question 1. Most of us introduce ourselves by saying what we do: My name is _____ and I'm a teacher, or a homemaker, or a computer programmer, or a mechanic. Encourage each member to respond.

Question 2. Those who are in Christ are blessed (v. 3), chosen, holy, blameless (v. 4), predestined (v. 5), a testimony to God's grace (v. 6), forgiven (v. 7), wise and understanding (v. 8), and marked with the Holy Spirit (v. 13). Lead your group to spot these and any other descriptions in the text, since they will be basic information for the rest of your discussion. In contrast with this letter, we typically think of ourselves in terms of what we do and not what we are. Help your group to discuss the difference.

Question 4. Paul gives these terms of traditional greeting new meaning by specifying God our Father and the Lord Jesus Christ as the source of both grace and peace. He uses them as a type of prayer for the believers. Perhaps combining the two greetings symbolized for Paul the unity which Jews and Gentiles now had in Christ.

Question 5. This may prove a difficult question. Help your group to study the text in order to better understand the mystery Paul describes. The mystery is God's plan to sum up all things in Christ (v. 10). It is a mystery in the sense that human intelligence could not have figured out what God planned to accomplish in Christ. The knowledge of this mystery is revealed to all who are in Christ. (Ephesians 3:3-6 has more on this topic.)

Question 6. Encourage a variety of responses here. Some people see God's foreknowledge or election as "fate," or an excuse for careless spirituality. Others stand in awe at God's power and are comforted by the knowledge that they rest in God's sure care. Paul responds in praise and awe of God. Some examples are: "praise be" (v. 3), "He chose us—to be holy" (v. 4), "He predestined us" (v. 5), "He has freely given" (v. 6), "the riches of God's grace" (v. 7), "He lavished on us" (v. 8).

Question 8. This question is meant to provide an opportunity for genuine self-examination, not to be a guilt-producer. Help group members to see the areas where they are demonstrating such understanding as well as those areas where God probably wants to transform their thinking.

Question 9. Refer to Elwell's *Evangelical Dictionary of Theology* for short definitions of words like predestination, salvation, and sanctification that your group can work with. Read these definitions for the group before discussing the answers. An example of the difference between our part and God's might be: salvation is initiated by God, there is nothing we can do to earn it because of the nature of our sin; sanctification is the process of our cooperating with the Holy Spirit to be conformed to the image of Christ. (Paul will get to our part in chapters 4–6.)

Study Three
Thanks and Praise
Ephesians 1:15-23

Purpose: To study how Paul bases his prayer for the Ephesians on what is true because they are "in Christ," so that we might do the same when we pray.

Question 1. Help people in your group to talk about their patterns of praying. Create an atmosphere where people can speak truthfully, not merely what they wish others to believe about their praying. On the other hand, be aware that this question can bring out valuable suggestions for intercessory prayer. Possible ways to pray might include: expressing appreciation to God for knowing these people for whom we pray, concern that they be mature in their faith, or that God will provide for their needs.

Question 2. Paul's first prayer for the Ephesians (there's another in chapter 3) is one of the most structurally complex prayers in all of Scripture. As a part of your personal preparation to lead, try writing the entire prayer in jotted outline form. This will help you see if group members cover all of the important concepts as they respond to this question. It will also give you a clear picture of how various phrases in the prayer relate to each other.

Along with other potential answers to this question, people should notice that Paul prays for wisdom and revelation in order that: we might know God (v. 17), be aware of all that we possess as children of God (v. 18), and experience the surpassing power of God which resides in all believers (v. 19). Help people in your group to compare their responses to question 1 with the way Paul prays for his readers.

Question 3. It is right to feel a continual concern for people God puts in our lives, praying frequently and sometimes over long periods of time. Since our needs are often ongoing (especially concerning our growth in wisdom and understanding of God), continual prayer is a necessity. Be prepared to share an example of how you have prayed for a person or concern over a period of time and any insights you gathered from that experience.

Question 4. After people have had a chance to express personal responses to this question, you may want to point out that we do indeed have someone praying for us who is far better than Paul— Jesus Christ Himself (Romans 8:26-27; Hebrews 7:23-25).

Question 5. None of us ever came to God of our own volition; our sin prevented us from being able to come to Him. God is the one who initiated toward us, giving us faith. We all stand in need of transformation in our hearts and minds in order to respond to God. You may want to mention to the group that Paul will soon remind his readers that, at one time, they were "dead" in their sins (2:1), but God made them "alive" out of His mercy (2:4). Paul is helping his readers to understand the magnitude of God's grace toward them.

Question 6. When Paul speaks of hope, he is not so much referring to a person's mood but equating it with the thing hoped for. His concepts of hope and riches have an eternal perspective expressed by Christ's resurrection as described in verse 20. To magnify your personal appreciation for this hope, try reading aloud to yourself Revelation 21.

Question 9. You may find it helpful to sketch the picture of Christ's authority that your group describes. Then let your group discuss the drawing or chart that emerges.

Question 10. The metaphor of "head" illustrates Christ's authority over, leadership of, and nurture of His "body," the church. (Paul further develops this aspect in Ephesians 4:15-16.) The image of "body" represents the church's subordination to, following of, and dependence upon Christ. The two images together depict the spiritual unity between Christ and the church as well as between believers.

Study Four
We're Either Alive or Dead
Ephesians 2:1-10

Purpose: To remember how we too were once dead in our sin, in order to be more grateful for the mercy God has shown us and to extend that mercy to others.

Question 1. This question is intended to help the members of your group appreciate Paul's choice of words in this passage, so encourage each person to respond.

Question 2. Paul describes those without Christ as: "dead" in sin (v. 1), following "the ways of this world" (v. 2), instruments of Satan (v. 2), gratifying the "cravings" of the sinful nature (v. 3), and "objects of wrath" (v. 3). Discuss any questions people may have concerning these descriptions. [*Note:* Since "objects of wrath" is discussed in question 4, hold any questions on that phrase until then.]

Question 4. The term "children of wrath" is a Hebrew expression. It refers to those who deserve God's judgment because of their sinful rebellion (see 5:6). It does not imply a fit of emotion against people.

Question 5. Allow the group to come up with their own answers to the question and then read the following: Many of the great Christian writers over the centuries have expressed wonder at the fact that God did not have to forgive any of us, but He freely chose to. God could have left us to suffer the consequences of our sin— and none of us could argue with His decision. Instead, God took on Himself the penalty for our sin, and this act of love and justice demonstrates the "incomparable riches of His grace."

Questions 6–7. Help your group to come up with several examples from each of the various media forms. Examples might include car commercials, fashion magazines, slogans: McDonalds's "You deserve a break today" or Burger King's "Have it your way." As you discuss these questions, your group may need to discern how to act responsibly in financial and personal ways, while still depending on God for spiritual well-being. It's okay to "earn our own way" when we buy a meal or a house. But we can't earn our own way with God. He gives us eternal life as a gift.

Your group may also discuss how we can acknowledge God's grace to us—even in our buying. Do we *deserve* a faster meal or a better car? If all that we have (including our ability to earn money) comes from God, the word "deserve" may not be an appropriate term.

Question 9. There are any number of ways to define a "good work." It might be a certain occupation, or a single act such as being kind to a stranger, or an ongoing work of serving your spouse/children/friends/parents/church. Even faith is a good work. Encourage each person in your group to respond to the question.

Question 10. Again, be sure each person has a chance to answer the question—since it will lead into your time of prayer.

Study Five
We Are One in the Spirit
Ephesians 2:11-22

Purpose: To appreciate how God in Christ has made a new humanity by joining Jews and Gentiles.

Question 3. If people are interested in the background of God's covenant with Israel, you can refer them to Genesis 15:1-21; 17:1-27; and 26:2-5.

Question 4. Paul clarifies this metaphor in verse 15 by referring to the Mosaic law. This law, which God established between Himself and the Israelites, kept His people separate and distinct from all other nations and prevented Gentiles from having access to God—since one's righteousness was judged by how well one fulfilled the requirements of the law. The physical structure of the temple vividly illustrated this separation, with its special court for the Gentiles and another for women.

Question 5. Your group should be able to come up with several examples. Some might include black vs. white, rich vs. poor, and charismatic vs. traditional.

Question 6. Have people in your group pick out answers from the text using references. Be sure to mention the following items if they do not on their own: Christ has united those with the law and those without it (v. 14) by destroying the need to fulfill the law's requirements (v. 15). He has made a new people, which includes both Jewish and Gentile believers (v. 15). He is both the maker (v. 14) and proclaimer (v. 17) of peace, and has become the door to a relationship with God (v. 18).

Question 7. Encourage people to think of similarities between how our own bodies function as a whole unit and how the church functions. For example, discrimination destroys the life of the church like a cancer that works its way throughout the body.

Question 8. Christ abolished the Law in that He perfectly fulfilled its requirements and took on Himself the penalty due those who disobeyed. He introduced a new age of righteousness, one based on faith, and thereby opened the way for Gentiles to be included. Now we obey God's commands (like the Ten Commandments) by the power of the Holy Spirit and not by our own strength alone.

Question 9. Have your group pick out points that speak to Gentile concerns and Jewish concerns. Help people to grasp the dynamic nature of the church, a living spiritual community in which God Himself dwells.

Study Six
Paul's Prayer for the Church
Ephesians 3:1-21

Purpose: To understand how God's work in human history has led to the establishment of the church, whose role it is to reveal God's wisdom to the world.

Question 1. Some possible reactions might be: grateful, indebted, unworthy, uncomfortable, motivated to make the most of my life. Encourage each person in your group to respond and to explain his or her answers.

Question 2. *Note:* When the Ephesians read about Paul's sufferings they probably felt some of the same emotions you discussed in question 1 (perhaps that was Paul's intention.) As you read chapter 3, keep the following organization in mind: Paul begins to pray for his readers (verses 1, 14-19), departs for a moment to explain why he calls himself a prisoner "for the sake of the Gentiles" (verses 2-13), and then praises God for His power (verses 20-21).

Paul says that he is in prison "for the sake of you Gentiles" (v. 1) and restates this in verse 13. He explains that God commissioned him to be their apostle (vv. 7-9), and that somehow he suffers for their "glory." Your group may find further explanations in verse 10 and even in the character of God expressed in the doxology of verses 20-21.

Question 3. In calling himself a "prisoner of Christ Jesus," Paul wasn't denying the fact that he was a Roman prisoner. Neither was he over-spiritualizing the situation. Since his imprisonment was a direct result of his ministry to the Gentiles, the expression reflects his heavenly perspective on his earthly circumstance. No one but Christ could claim to have control or power over him, and this knowledge probably brought him great comfort.

Question 5. We don't know why God chose to reveal His intention over time and not all at once. Still, it is worth reflecting on the fact, if only to marvel at God's surpassing wisdom and awesome accomplishments throughout human history.

Question 6. Make sure the group's reflections center around the message of Ephesians, and don't take off on unprofitable tangents.

Question 7. Concerning how Paul prayed: he knelt before God (v. 14). Jews normally stood to pray; kneeling indicated urgency or distress. By kneeling, Paul showed that he took his calling to the Gentiles seriously. He also prayed to the Father, the distinctively Christian name for God that Jesus used when he prayed. Concerning what Paul prayed: He prayed that they would be strengthened spiritually (v. 16) in order to believe in Christ (v. 17); grounded in love (v. 17); and empowered to know fully, together with all believers, the surpassing love of Christ (vv. 18-19).

Question 8. As your group discusses this question, it should come to these or similar conclusions: Our knowing is not only a matter of intellectual understanding, though it is that. We are to know God in the sense of being personally acquainted with Him, experiencing His reality in our daily lives. Paul's paradoxical language expresses the fact that we can always know more of God's love—it is inexhaustible.

Question 9. Allow the members in your group to come up with answers on their own. If it is not mentioned, read the following: While Paul is saying that we can never ask too much from God because His capacity to give far exceeds our ability to ask, the context of our asking is Paul's prayer in verses 16-19: the knowledge of God. This is what God gives us so abundantly.

Study Seven
United We Stand
Ephesians 4:1-16

Purpose: To understand the kind of unity the church is called to and why.

Question 1. This question is designed to help your group appreciate why Paul organizes his letter as he did. He bases his exhortations to live godly lives on the reality that we have been made alive in Christ and are now dead to sin. Like a football coach with his players before the championship game or a dance instructor before a performance, a good pep talk imparts a vision of who the people are at their best and where they are destined to go.

Question 2. Before this passage is read aloud, ask your group to keep in mind the first three chapters of the letter—the various ways Paul has already described his readers. In this chapter, Paul says that people living a life worthy of their calling (v. 1) are characterized by humility, gentleness, patience (v. 2), and unity among believers (v. 3).

Question 3. Unity in the church testifies to the reality of God, that He has dealt with the problem of sin and has brought together people from all nations, cultures, and classes. There have always been misunderstandings in the church about what true Christian unity means, so take some time to allow people to discuss and respond to each other's questions about what unity is and what it is not. The kind of unity Paul is referring to is explained in verses 4-6; it is the oneness of God and not some sort of shared community experience or identical functions. Verse 11 describes a variety of gifts that define function within that unity.

Question 5. First, God gives believers grace to accomplish His purposes. Second, all believers are given gifts to exercise in the church. Third, it is Christ who gives the gifts. The particular gifts Paul isolates here in Ephesians come in the form of people, ministers of the Word. It may be helpful to note the gifts mentioned in 1 Corinthians 12 and Romans 12, to show that none of these lists is exhaustive.

Question 6. You may want to refer people to Acts 2 (especially verse 33) to review the event of Pentecost. Christ has filled all things in that He has given all that He has from God (power, gifts, grace) to the church—so that it can continue His work.

Question 7. The purpose of Christ's gifts is to equip His people to serve in order to build up the body of Christ. The goal is spiritual maturity, becoming like Christ.

Question 9. It is worth noting that in American culture, where we value individualism above almost everything else, Paul's exhortation to submit, forbear, and work together for God's sake and not our own is revolutionary. It is not easy—as anyone who has served for a time in the church will attest. Some Christians do not see the importance of regularly worshiping in a local church, let alone being committed to diligently serving its members. Help your group to grasp the picture Paul is presenting of the counter-cultural (and counter-human!) way the church is meant to function. Encourage each person to measure his or her current beliefs about the church by what is being taught in Ephesians 4:1-16.

Study Eight
Created to Be Like God
Ephesians 4:17-32

Purpose: To understand that certain behavior among believers is necessary to maintain the unity of the church.

Question 2. Have your group go through the passage looking first for descriptions of those controlled by sin (you may want to spend some time discussing the meaning of the phrase "hardening of their hearts" in verse 18). Then go through it again for the marks of those controlled by the Spirit. Your group should find a dozen or more for each. Tie in any relevant comments from your discussion of question 1.

Question 3. This is a tough question because it is one of those "already" but "not yet" aspects of our Christian experience: a Christian is one who is "already" forgiven his/her sins and stands clean before God, but the reality of this change is "not yet" fully realized—not until heaven. When a person is converted he or she is cleansed from the controlling power of sin and receives the Holy Spirit to be able to live a life that pleases God. But, although sin no longer controls the Christian, it can still tempt. Putting off our old self is part of the gradual process of being made like Christ.

Question 4. It is a lifelong work to keep from being conformed to our surroundings, just as you already discussed in question 3. We all have stories of what happens when we become spiritually lazy or naive about the world's influence on us.

Question 6. Have two or three people volunteer to answer. If no one volunteers, be prepared to share your own ideas to get the discussion going.

Question 8. Jesus said that He is the truth (John 14:6) and that

His truth sets us free (John 8:32). What we *believe* does make a difference in how we live. But to live in a way that is pleasing to God and loving toward others requires a fundamental change inside (conversion), and this is radically different from the approach of many education and rehabilitation programs.

Question 9. In general, the "do not" commands reflect a life of deceit and corruption; they tear down and destroy. In contrast, the "do" commands reflect a life of truth and holiness; they seek to support and strengthen. Paul's message of unity (vv. 1-6) is promoted by the corporate expression of these virtues. Your group may also notice the practical connection between "speaking the truth in love" (v. 15) with the more specific instructions in verses 25-26.

Study Nine
Light in the Darkness
Ephesians 5:1-20

Purpose: To examine what it means and looks like to be distinctly different from unbelievers.

Question 2. Verse 1 is a continuation of 4:32, which spoke of God forgiving us. When Paul says "therefore," he means that we are to imitate God's forgiveness as children imitate their parents. Your group should spot the phrase "God's holy people" in verse 3 and also "inheritance in the kingdom," in verse 5. People will also find a host of phrases in verses 1-2, 8-10, 14-15, and 18-20.

Question 3. Children of light are characterized by lives of sacrificial love. Children of darkness live in self-indulgent sensuality. Paul's language in verse 3 connotes general sexual immorality. Note to your group the consequence of such a life as explained in verse 5. This is a contrast to 1:14, 18.

Question 5. Paul is giving them a positive reason for not engaging in sins: they are being changed by God! This behavior is to conform with their identity.

Question 6. Your group should first answer this question from implications found in the text. (Verses 8-10 may prove especially helpful.) Then expand to personal observations and experience. The very presence of a Christian can illumine a person's sinful behavior. The distinctive life of the Christian ought to stand in stark contrast to that of the unbeliever. This can be either threatening or win-some — Jesus had both effects on people. If unbelievers take offense at us, it should be because of Christ's presence in us and not any offensive traits such as pride or hypocrisy. After all, Paul reminds his readers in verse 8 that they too were once darkness. To be in a position to expose sin, Christians must be above reproach them-selves and they must also associate with people who are in darkness. The light Christ gives His people is meant to purify us and to be light to others.

Question 7. The scriptural practice of confessing our sins has a specific purpose: to lead us to repentance. Sharing one's secret thoughts and practices indiscriminately, although it may make a person feel better, does not have this purpose in mind. What we hear affects how we think, which in turn affects how we behave. Not participating in this kind of conversation is a way of protecting the integrity and unity of the body of Christ.

Study Ten
As unto the Lord
Ephesians 5:21-33

Purpose: To grasp the high calling of marriage and how God intends it for our benefit as well as His glory.

Question 2. Paul says that husbands and wives are to submit to God's design for marriage (that is, submitting and loving) out of reverence for Christ (v. 21). Because of the potential for difference of opinion over these verses it may be helpful to underscore what Paul is teaching here (and what he is not) by continually bringing the group's discussion back to the text for answers. The context here is marriage between two believers who are committed to serv-ing Christ. When Paul wrote the instructions here to husbands and wives, he assumed the context of a loving, Christ-centered relationship. Paul gives instructions concerning marriage to unbelievers in 1 Corinthians 7.

Question 3. Since Paul's instruction here is to wives, invite the women in your group to answer the question first. Christ gives to the wife the responsibility to subordinate herself to the loving authority of her husband. Submitting to her husband in this way is how she demonstrates her submission to Christ (v. 21). She is called to voluntary self-renunciation. Ask your group to page back through Ephesians for help in understanding Paul's use thus far of the submission concept. People can discuss the concepts in 4:2-3, 7, 25-26, 28-29, 32; 5:1-2, and others.

An example of a misunderstanding of submission is to see the wife as someone who does not think for herself but simply does whatever her husband tells her. Some Christian homes have misapplied this passage in this way and the result has been abuse. Husbands also are harmed by this kind of misuse of the text because their wives have so squelched their own desires and ideas that they have inadvertently nurtured their husbands into complacent selfishness.

Question 4. Since Paul's instruction here is to husbands, invite the men in your group to answer the question first. Christ gives to the husband the responsibility to love his wife in a way that selflessly nurtures and fosters her relationship with Christ. Loving his wife in this way is how he demonstrates his submission to Christ (v. 21). He is called to voluntary self-renunciation. Some important differences between the husband and our Lord are: the husband is unlike Christ in that he is not the creator, sustainer, or redeemer of his wife.

Question 7. Encourage the women and men in your group to share reactions to the particular instruction addressed to them. Be careful to facilitate the flow of discussion so that tough questions and issues may be voiced without dominating or digressing from the passage at hand.

Question 8. Because of sin, the marriage relationship is now impaired by inclinations toward abuse of its authority structure. (Compare this text with Genesis 4:7 where the same idea is found.)

Study Eleven
Children and Parents/Slaves and Masters
Ephesians 6:1-9

Purpose: To see how God desires that not only our marriages but also our families and work relationships be characterized by our submission to Christ.

Question 2. Paul continues to develop their understanding that no matter what their social position (child/parent, slave/master), their motivation in all circumstances is to serve Christ. In this way they will maintain their unity as members of Christ's body—the theme Paul has been developing throughout his letter.

Question 3. Common sense, as well as Scripture, tells us that the honor/obedience we give to our parents is limited by the honor we owe to God. This is important to remember in the event we are asked to do anything which is contrary to God's commands. The brief phrase "in the Lord" (v. 1) helps establish this caution. Your group may think of specific examples or circumstances where we can honor our parents—even if we cannot obey them. Parents should not, of course, expect children who have grown to adulthood to continue to obey them. Honor, however, is another matter.

Question 5. If your group is having difficulty answering the question, encourage them to look at the preceding verses for clues. (This is always a good way to understand a particular passage because it helps the reader to see the author's train of thought.) It may be that, in the same way Paul notes husbands' unique responsibility before God for the well-being of their wives, fathers also are responsible to exercise their God-given authority in a way that nurtures the development of their children into mature Christians.

If you need follow-up questions ask: *What does Paul's instruction to fathers imply about the role of parenting? What does it imply about the nature of children?* If you use these questions, your group will likely discover that Paul says it is primarily the responsibility of the parents, not the church, to bring up their children in the faith. This has implications for how churches function in their training of parents to in turn train their children, as well as for the goals of church education programs.

Concerning the nature of children, one might argue that this passage demonstrates that: (1) children need to be given direction from their parents and are not to be left to their own search for faith when they are young, and (2) this exercise of authority is an expression of the parents' love for their children, in that they recognize their children's need for guidance and provide it. People in your group can pool their resources to discuss a variety of practical ways to bring this about.

Question 7. Paul reminds his readers of the fact that there is one Master for both the slave and the earthly master, and this fact ought to affect how both of them go about their work—as slaves of Christ.

We might wonder why Paul encouraged slaves to "obey" their masters (that is, not revolt), instead of working to change the system. But what was truly radical to Paul's readers was that he addressed slaves as fellow members in the body of Christ—on equal footing with their masters before God! It is possible that churches of the first century contained elders who were slaves and masters who were not elders. If so, how might these people have related to each other while on the job? While in the church? How would Paul's commands here have helped them? This "same family" relationship would have revolutionized the normal practice of slavery.

Question 8. One difference is that Paul was addressing believers and many of us work with unbelievers. Also, our democratic style of management and labor relations are not equivalent to the first-century system of slavery. Be sure that your group discusses similarities as well as differences.

Question 9. The principle of doing everything as if you were serving the Lord, not human beings (v. 7) applies to believers in all generations. Your group may find other principles as well in this passage. Draw from all of verses 1-9. Answers here will form a basis for your closing discussion in question 10, so be as thorough as necessary for good preparation.

Study Twelve
To Arms!
Ephesians 6:10-24

Purpose: To see how the battle between Satan and God has already been won but that believers must wear their spiritual armor until Christ's victory is fully realized.

Question 1. Members in your group may hold different views on the devil and how he and his angels work to thwart God's people. Possible views are: Satan is a personal being who marshals evil forces and influences people to do wrong, or Satan is an impersonal force that influences people to do his bidding, or that Satan doesn't exist; people make their own choices about right and wrong. Try to allow the *text* to be the judge of any differing views as you discuss this passage.

Question 2. Your group should cite such phrases as "devil's schemes" (v. 11), "not ... flesh and blood" (v. 12), "spiritual forces of evil" (v. 12), "in the heavenly realms" (v. 12), he will cause a "day of evil" (v. 13), and "flaming arrows of the evil one" (v. 16). As people point out these descriptions, discuss what they mean. Have your group draw implications about Satan's power and work based on the kinds of defense that God provides. For example, there is no equipment to protect a believer's back; we must fight our spiritual enemy with spiritual weapons (vv. 10, 12); the armor is essential to our survival and includes all the resources necessary to resist the devil (v. 13).

Note: The term "heavenly realms" has its nearest parallel in 2:2. Both texts locate the Christian's battle in the region (not specified) where Christ rules, which explains the "therefore" of verse 13.

Question 4. See Guthrie's *New Bible Commentary* for interesting insights on the pieces of armor.

Question 7. When Paul calls believers to "pray in the Spirit," he means prayer that is guided and inspired and made effective by the Holy Spirit. Refer to 2:18, 22; 5:18 to see how Paul builds his case.

Question 8. Your group should spot such key phrases in the text as "words may be given me" (Paul did much of the writing that has defined Christianity for 2,000 years during this stay in prison), "fearlessly" (mentioned twice), "make known the mystery of the Gospel," "ambassador" (for Christ), and "in chains." With these responsibilities and circumstances, it is small wonder that Paul requested prayer.

Question 9. The battle is over, and God is the victor. These are certainties that can comfort believers in the midst of trials and temptations. That is what the "Therefore" of verse 13 implies. Remember, Paul's first three chapters were all about what God has accomplished for us in Christ.

Question 11. Your group should draw on information throughout these closing verses. They speak not only of Paul's relationship with the Ephesians but also his relationship with the Tychicus and also with God. Some sharp-eyed reader may notice that Paul closes his letter with the same blessing with which he began: "Grace and peace be with you."

For Further Reading

Aharoni, Yohanan, and Michael Avi-Yonah, eds. *The MacMillan Bible Atlas.* Revised Edition. New York and London: Collier MacMillan Publishers, 1977.

Barth, Markus. *Ephesians.* Anchor Bible. 2 vols. Garden City, NY: Doubleday & Co., Inc., 1974.

Bright, John. *A History of Israel.* 3rd ed. Philadelphia: The Westminster Press, 1981.

Bromiley, Geoffrey W., ed. *International Standard Bible Encyclopedia.* 4 vols. Grand Rapids: Eerdmans, 1982.

Douglas, J.D., F.F. Bruce, J.I. Packer, N. Hilyer, D. Guthrie, A.R. Millard, and D.J. Wiseman, eds. *New Bible Dictionary.* 2nd ed. Leicester, England: Inter-Varsity Press, 1982.

Ellis, E. Earle. "Pseudonimity and Canonicity of New Testament Documents." in *Worship, Theology and Ministry in the Early Church: Essays in honor of Ralph P. Martin,* Michael J. Wilkins and Terence Paige, eds. Sheffield, England: JSOT Press, 1992.

Elwell, Walter A., ed. *Evangelical Dictionary of Theology.* Grand Rapids: Baker, 1984.

Fee, Gordon, and Douglas Stuart. *How to Read the Bible for All It's Worth.* Grand Rapids: Zondervan, 1982.

Ferguson, Sinclair B. and David F. Wright, eds. *New Dictionary of Theology.* Downers Grove, IL and Leicester, England: Inter-Varsity Press, 1988.

Finzel, Hans. *Observe Interpret Apply: How to Study the Bible Inductively.* Wheaton, IL: Victor Books, 1994.

Gorman, Julie A. *Community That is Christian: A Handbook for Small Groups.* Wheaton, IL: Victor Books, 1993.

Guthrie, Donald. *New Testament Introduction.* Rev. ed. Downers Grove, Ill.: InterVarsity Press, 1992.

Guthrie, Donald, et al. *The New Bible Commentary: Revised.* Grand Rapids: Zondervan, 1970.

Kuhatschek, Jack. *Taking the Guesswork out of Applying the Bible.* Downers Grove, IL: InterVarsity Press, 1990.

Lawrence, Brother and Donald C. Demaray. *The Practice of the Presence of God.* Grand Rapids: Baker, 1975.

Lewis, C.S. *Mere Christianity.* New York: MacMillan Publishing, 1960.

———. *The Weight of Glory.* 1980.

———. *Mere Christianity.* 1982.

Lincoln, Andrew T. *Ephesians. Word Biblical Commentary.* Dallas: Word, 1990.

Plueddemann, Jim and Carol. *Pilgrims in Progress: Growing through Groups.* Wheaton, IL: Harold Shaw Publishers, 1990.

Tasker, R.V.G., ed. *Tyndale New Testament Commentaries,* 20 vols. Grand Rapids: Eerdmans, 1963–1980.

Tenney, Merrill C., ed. *The Zondervan Pictorial Encyclopedia of the Bible.* 5 vols. Grand Rapids, MI: Zondervan, 1975, 1976.

Walvoord, John F., and Roy B. Zuck, eds. *The Bible Knowledge Commentary, New Testament Edition.* Wheaton, Ill.: Victor, 1983.

Wenham, G.J., J.A. Motyer, D.A. Carson, and R.T. France, eds. *New Bible Commentary: 21st Century Edition.* Downers Grove, IL and Leicester, England: InterVarsity Press. 1994.

Wuthnow, Robert. *Sharing the Journey: Support Groups and America's New Quest for Community.* New York: The Free Press, 1994.

Notes and Prayers

About the Author

In work and play Patti Picardi enjoys juggling several interests at a time, trying to maintain a balance between thinking about life and experiencing it—and she always finds something to laugh about. Seeing God in the circumstances of life is her passion, and she loves to share that passion with others. Thus her choice of Ephesians.

Patti comes alive when she's outdoors, whether it's playing church-league softball, hiking in the White Mountains of New Hampshire, or walking along the beach. Having lived on Long Island Sound for fifteen years (sailing many of those summers) her favorite memories revolve around the ocean. She says that the rhythm of the tides, the terror of the swells, the surprise of storms, and the lullaby of the waves imprinted something of God's nature on her soul.

Patti holds a B.A. in International Relations from Bucknell University and an M.A. in Theological Studies from Gordon-Conwell Theological Seminary. She works as a freelance editor and writer in South Hamilton, Massachusetts.